AQA GCSE
(9–1)
Physics

Required Practicals Lab Book

Emily Quinn

William Collins' dream of knowledge for all began with the publication of his first book in 1819. A self-educated mill worker, he not only enriched millions of lives, but also founded a flourishing publishing house. Today, staying true to this spirit, Collins books are packed with inspiration, innovation and practical expertise. They place you at the centre of a world of possibility and give you exactly what you need to explore it.

Collins. Freedom to teach

Published by Collins
An imprint of HarperCollins*Publishers*
The News Building
1 London Bridge Street
London SE1 9GF

Browse the complete Collins catalogue at
www.collins.co.uk

© HarperCollins*Publishers* Limited 2018

10 9

ISBN 978-0-00-829163-1

British Library Cataloguing in Publication Data
A catalogue record for this publication is available from the British Library.

Author: Emily Quinn
Commissioning editor: Rachael Harrison
In-house project editor: Isabelle Sinclair
Copyeditor and typesetter: Hugh Hillyard-Parker
Proofreader and answer checker: Tim Jackson
Artwork: QBS Learning
Cover designer: Julie Martin
Cover photo: © anuj88chawla/Shutterstock.com
Production controller: Tina Paul
Printed and bound by: Martins the Printers, Berwick-upon-Tweed

MIX
Paper from
responsible sources
FSC www.fsc.org **FSC™ C007454**

This book is produced from independently certified FSC™ Paper to ensure responsible forest management.

For more information visit: www.harpercollins.co.uk/green

The publishers will gladly receive any information enabling them to rectify any error or omission at the first opportunity.

Contents

Practical skills are at the heart of any science qualification. Your AQA GCSE Science course requires you to develop these skills through completing a series of required practicals, which you will then be tested on in your exams. This lab book will help you record the results of your practical work, and provide you with some guidance so that you get the most out of your time completing each practical.

Ensure you write down everything you can about your practical work – remember you can refer back to this book when you're revising!

Learning outcomes

This is a summary of what you should have accomplished by the end of each required practical.

Apparatus list

Your teacher will ensure that all the apparatus you need for the practical can be found in the classroom. You can use this list to check that you have everything you need to start your work.

Maths skills required

This is a good reminder of the skills you will need to master and practise on your science course, which will be tested in your exams. There are also questions included throughout that let you practise your maths skills.

Formulae

Any formulae you need to know to complete your practical work are shown here. A full list of formulae can be found on pages 47 and 48.

Safety notes

You should always be aware of safety when completing any practical work. This list will help you be aware of any common safety issues. Your teacher will advise on safety information for each practical, so pay attention.

Common mistakes

We've included some of the common mistakes people make during their practical work so that you can look out for them and hopefully avoid making the same mistakes.

Method

Always make sure you read every step of the method before you begin work. This will help you avoid mistakes and will give you an idea of what outcomes to look for as you complete each step.

Record your results

At the end of every method is place to record the outcomes of your work. Make sure you keep your notes clear and neat.

Check your understanding and Exam-style questions

For each practical, there are questions designed to check your understanding of the work you've just completed. There are also exam-style questions, which are included to help you prepare for questions in the exam. Some of these questions are designed to test your maths skills and to check your understanding of the apparatus and techniques that you've been using, as you'll be tested on these aspects of practical work in your exams.

Higher Tier

HT If you see this symbol next to a question, then it is designed for Higher Tier content only.

Teachers should always ensure they consult the latest CLEAPSS safety guidance before undertaking any practical work.

4.1.1.3 Specific heat capacity

In this practical you will measure the temperature changes of different materials when they are heated so you can calculate their specific heat capacity. This investigation involves linking the decrease of one energy store (or work done) to the increase in thermal energy stored. The energy transferred (work done) will cause a temperature rise.

In this investigation, the temperature rise of a material depends on its **specific heat capacity**. Materials with a low specific heat capacity (a low capacity to store thermal energy) will have a greater temperature increase than those with a high specific heat capacity.

Learning outcomes	Maths skills required	Formulae
• Safely collect data to calculate the specific heat capacity of a metal block, or of water. • Understand how to identify any anomalous results.	• Substitute numerical values into algebraic equations using appropriate units for physical quantities. • Plot two variables from experimental data. • Determine the slope of a linear graph.	• change in thermal energy (J) = mass (kg) × specific heat capacity (J/kg °C) × change in temperature (°C) $\Delta E = mc\Delta\theta$ • energy transferred (J) = power (W) × time (s) power (W) = • potential difference (V) × current (A)

Apparatus list

- copper block with two holes, for a thermometer and a heater
- aluminium block with two holes, for a thermometer and a heater
- 250 cm³ beaker
- water
- thermometer
- petroleum jelly
- 50 W, 12 V heater

- 12 V power supply
- insulation to wrap around the block or beaker
- ammeter
- voltmeter
- five leads
- stopwatch
- balance (mass)
- eye protection

Safety notes

- Wear eye protection at all times.
- Be careful with water around electricity.
- The heating element will get very hot, especially if it is not inside a metal block. Take care not to burn yourself.
- If any of the equipment is damaged do not use it.
- If you scald yourself with hot water, cool the burn under cold running water immediately and ask your teacher for assistance.

Common mistakes

- The heating element should fit very snugly into the metal block, but there may be a small layer of air between the heating element and the metal block. Add a drop of water before you put the heating element in to improve transfer of energy between the heating element and the metal block.

- Remember to measure the mass of the metal block. These blocks are usually 1 kg, but to make sure your calculations are accurate, you should take an accurate mass measurement.

- Your teacher might tell you the power of your heater. You can trust your teacher, or you can attach an ammeter and voltmeter and calculate the power using:

   power (W) = potential difference (V) × current (A)
   $P = VI$

- Make sure you heat the metal block for at least 10 minutes; otherwise you will not be able to draw a graph with a good range of results.

- Don't forget to use your graph to find the gradient of the line. You will need this and the mass of the block to work out the specific heat capacity of your metals.

Method

Read these instructions carefully before you start work.

1. Choose your material, for example, a copper or aluminium block, and measure its mass, in kilograms. (Note: if choosing water, first find the mass of the beaker, then the mass of the beaker and the water, then subtract the mass of the beaker to determine the mass of the water.)

2. Wrap insulation around your block or beaker.

3. Smear petroleum jelly around the bulb end of the thermometer (not necessary if measuring temperature of water rather than of metal block) then put the thermometer in the small hole in the block (or into the water).

4. Measure the starting temperature of the block (or water).

Figure 1

5. Put a heater in the larger hole in the block. Connect the ammeter, power pack and heater in series, as shown in **Figure 1**.

6. Connect the voltmeter across the power pack, as shown in **Figure 1**.

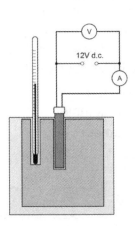

7. Turn the power pack to 12 V and switch it on. Start the stopwatch as you turn on the power pack.

8. Record the ammeter and voltmeter readings every 60 seconds in **Table 1**. These may vary slightly during the experiment, but not significantly. Record the temperature of the metal block (or water) every 60 seconds in **Table 2**. If you are using water, stir it at regular intervals.

9. After 10 minutes, turn off the power pack.

10. Keep the thermometer in the metal block (or water) for a while longer. Record the **maximum** temperature of the metal block (or water) in **Table 2** – this may be a little while after you have turned off the power pack.

11. Calculate the power of the heater and record the values in **Table 1**. Then calculate the energy transferred (work done) up to each time point. Use the following equations:
   power (W) = potential difference (V) × current (A)
   energy transferred (J) = power (W) × time (s)

12. Plot your results on **Graph 1**, with temperature change (°C) on the y-axis and energy transferred (J) on the x-axis.

Record your results

Table 1 – Calculating power

Time (s)	Potential difference (V)	Current (A)	Power (W)
0			
60			
120			
180			
240			
300			
360			
420			
480			
540			
600			

Table 2 – Calculating energy transferred

Time (s)	Energy transferred (J)	Temperature of metal block (°C)
0		
60		
120		
180		
240		
300		
360		
420		
480		
540		
600		
Maximum temperature of block		

Graph 1

Theory suggests that the specific heat capacity can be found from:

$$\text{specific heat capacity} = \frac{1}{\text{mass} \times \text{gradient}}$$

Use your graph and this equation to determine the specific heat capacity of your metal.

....

Check your understanding

1. It is important to stir the water regularly when heating the water. Explain why.   [1 mark]

....

2. A student repeats the experiment for a block of copper four times.

   The results for the temperature of the block after 10 minutes are: 87 °C, 71 °C, 68 °C and 69 °C.

   a. Calculate the mean maximum temperature. Take into account any anomalous results.
                                                                                                          [2 marks]

   ....

   ....

b. Give one reason why the student may have anomalous results. [1 mark]

....

3. If the heating element is not in contact with the metal block, there will be a layer of air in between the heating element and the metal block. The calculated specific heat capacity may then be **greater** than the actual value.

Explain why. [1 mark]

....

4. Another method to calculate specific heat capacity of an object is to immerse the object in ice cold water until the object reaches 0 °C and then to place it in a beaker of hotter water.

In **Figure 2**, a brass block is moved from water at 0 °C to hot water at 80 °C.

Figure 2

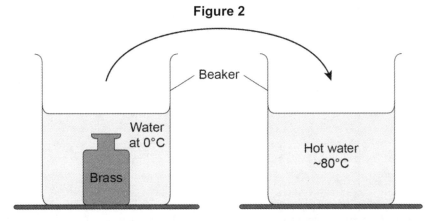

List three pieces of equipment that would be needed to calculate the specific heat capacity of the brass. [3 marks]

....

....

Exam-style questions

1. 1 kg of aluminium was heated for 10 minutes.
Table 3 shows the results.

Table 3

Energy transferred (J)	Temperature (°C)
0	23
4500	28
9000	33
13 500	38
18 000	43
22 500	48
27 000	53

a. Complete **Graph 2** using data from **Table 3**.

• Plot the additional data points.

• Draw a line of best fit. [3 marks]

Graph 2

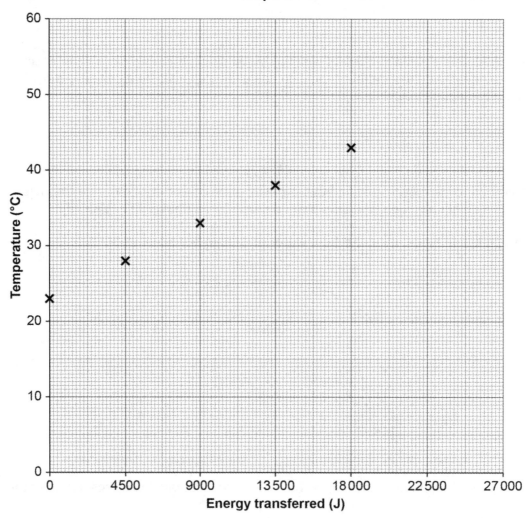

Energy transferred (J)

b. Determine the specific heat capacity of <u>this block</u> of aluminium. Use the gradient of the line and the formula below.

$$\text{specific heat capacity} = \frac{1}{\text{mass} \times \text{gradient}}$$

[2 marks]

....

....

2. The specific heat capacity for three different metals is listed in **Table 4**.

Table 4

Metal	Specific heat capacity (J/kg °C)
Aluminium	897
Copper	385
Iron	450

All three materials are commonly used as cooking pans. Which material would heat up the fastest? Give a reason for your answer.   [2 marks]

....

....

4.1.2.1 Thermal insulation

Energy will always be transferred from warmer places to cooler ones. Sometimes this is useful, as in a domestic heating system. However, on other occasions we need to stop that transfer, or at least slow it down. In this investigation you will study the rate of cooling of a beaker of hot water when insulated with different thicknesses of insulating materials. You will plot cooling curves to determine if there is any benefit in using additional layers for thermal insulation.

Learning outcomes	Maths skills required
• Identify variables that need to be kept constant in order to ensure validity of results. • Plot a graph of the results and use it to compare the rates of cooling.	• Translate information between graphical and numeric form. • Plot two variables from experimental data.

Apparatus list	
• beaker (for example, 250 cm^3) • thermometer • electric kettle (and water) • piece of cardboard • scissors	• stopwatch • insulating material of different thicknesses or enough to have numbers of layers • rubber bands

Safety notes
• Do not handle the electric kettle, plug or socket with wet hands. • If you scald yourself with hot water, cool the burn under cold running water immediately and ask your teacher for assistance.

Common mistakes
• Make sure the thermometer is actually in the water. • Make sure you use the same volume of water each time.

Method

Read these instructions carefully before you start work.

1.   Set up 6 beakers, with 0, 1, 2, 3, 4 and 5 layers of insulating material around each beaker. Each group will use a different beaker.

2.   Pour 200 cm^3 of hot water into your beaker.

3.   Use a piece of cardboard, with a hole for the thermometer, as a lid for the beaker.

4.   Push the thermometer through the hole in the cardboard lid so that its bulb is in the hot water.

5.   Measure the temperature of the hot water and record this in **Table 1** in the correct row for your number of layers. **Start the stopwatch**.

6.   Every 5 minutes measure the temperature of the water and record it in **Table 1**.

7.   Continue for 20 minutes.

8.   Record the class results in **Table 1**.

9.   Draw cooling curve graphs by plotting **temperature (°C)** against **time (s)** for each number of different layers of insulation on **Graph 1**. Draw the curves for each number of layers on the same graph.

10. From your graph, write a conclusion about the effect of changing the number of layers of insulation.

11. To compare the insulating material with other materials, repeat your experiment with a different material or compare your results with your peers if they have used a different material. Record your results in a copy of **Table 1** and stick it into your book.

Record your results

Table 1 – Number of layers and temperature

Number of layers	Temperature (°C)				
	0 mins	5 mins	10 mins	15 mins	20 mins
0					
1					
2					
3					
4					
5					

Graph 1

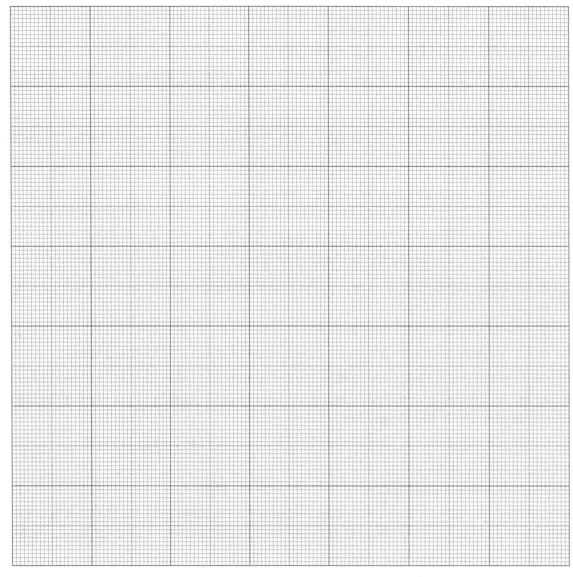

Conclusion

Check your understanding

1. The graph you have drawn should have six curves on it.

   a. Describe the general trend of all the curves on your graph. [2 marks]

   ....

   ....

   b. How many layers would be the most appropriate to keep a beaker of water warm for longest? Use data from your results to support your answer. [3 marks]

   ....

   ....

   ....

   ....

2. Explain why the same volume of water was used each time. [2 marks]

   ....

   ....

3. A student wants to keep ice cream frozen when the ice cream is outside the freezer.

   How many layers of insulation you would advise the student to use?

   Explain why you would advise this many layers. [3 marks]

   ....

   ....

   ....

Exam-style questions

1. **Table 2** shows a student's results after an experiment investigating the insulating properties of different materials.

Table 2

Thermal insulator	Temperature of the pot (°C)					
	Start	1 hour	2 hours	3 hours	4 hours	5 hours
Cling film	90.0	38.0	26.5	25.5	25.0	25.0
Bubble wrap	90.0	43.5	28.0	25.5	25.5	25.0
Polystyrene	90.0	55.0	43.5	37.5	30.0	26.5
Wood shavings	90.0	52.5	40.0	32.5	28.0	25.5

a. Describe a method the student could have used to collect this data.

You should include the safety precautions the student should take. [6 marks]

....

....

....

....

....

....

....

....

....

....

....

....

b. Explain why the lowest temperature reached is 25 °C. [1 mark]

....

We can use an electrical circuit to determine the resistance of a component, as resistance can be calculated from measurements of potential difference and current. We can then see how the resistance is affected by factors such as the length of a wire or when several components are combined.

A dimmer switch is a device that alters the resistance of a circuit and allows you to control the brightness of a lamp. You will investigate the principle of how a dimmer switch works. You will construct a circuit to measure the potential difference across a wire and the current through the wire. You will do this for different lengths of wire and for resistors in series and in parallel.

Learning outcomes	Maths skills required	Formulae
<ul><li>Set up a circuit to investigate resistance.</li><li>Make measurements using ammeters and voltmeters.</li><li>Use circuit diagrams to construct and check series and parallel circuits.</li></ul>	<ul><li>Display experimental data in a suitable table.</li><li>Plot two variables from experimental data.</li><li>Understand that $y = mx + c$ represents a linear relationship.</li><li>Understand and use the symbol $\propto$</li><li>Use an appropriate number of significant figures.</li></ul>	<ul><li>$V = IR$</li><li>resistance = potential difference ÷ current $R = \dfrac{V}{I}$</li></ul>

Apparatus list

- d.c. power supply
- voltmeter
- ammeter
- length of resistance wire mounted on a metre rule
- connecting leads
- crocodile clips
- two 10 Ω resistors
- eye protection
- ohmmeter (if available)

Safety notes

- Short lengths of wire are likely to get hot. Use low values of potential difference. Switch off between readings.
- You can add a bulb to your circuit to stop the wire from getting too hot.

Common mistakes

- If your readings keep fluctuating, try to get an average value. Ammeters and voltmeters rarely stay at an exact value.

Methods

Read these instructions carefully before you start work.

There are two activities in this practical.

Activity 1 – Investigating how the length of a wire affects resistance

1. Set up the circuit as shown in **Figure 1**. The rectangle (symbol for a resistor) is where you should place the component that is being tested.

2. Attach your component, a metre rule with a wire, where the resistor symbol is. Use crocodile clips to add this component in to your circuit as shown in **Figure 2**.

Figure 1

0–12 V d.c.

Figure 2

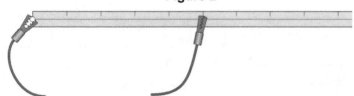

3. Place the crocodile clips so they are 100 cm apart.

4. Turn on the power pack at 4 V.

   Measure both the potential difference across the wire and the current through the wire. Record these results in **Table 1**.

5. **Turn off the power pack**.

   Reduce the length of the wire between the crocodile clips by 10 cm.

6. Repeat steps **4** and **5** for all wire lengths down to 10 cm.

   Be careful – the wire may get hot. Turn off the power pack if the wire starts glowing or smoking.

7. Calculate the resistance for each length of wire using the formula:

   resistance = potential difference ÷ current $R = \dfrac{V}{I}$

   Record the values of resistance in **Table 1**.

8. Plot a graph of resistance against length of wire in the space for **Graph 1**:

   - **Resistance in Ω** on the *y*-axis
   - **Length of wire in cm** on the *x*-axis.

Activity 2 – Investigating resistors in series and in parallel

1. Set up the circuit shown in **Figure 1** with two resistors in series where the rectangle is.

2. Turn on the power pack at 4 V.

3. Measure the potential difference across the power pack.

4. Measure the potential difference across each individual resistor and the current through them.

5. Calculate the total resistance of the circuit with resistors in series.

6. Set up the circuit for two resistors in parallel.

7. Repeat steps **2–4** for the resistors in parallel.

8. Calculate the total resistance of the circuit with resistors in parallel.

Record your results

Table 1 – Calculating resistance

Length of wire (cm)	Current (A)	Potential difference (V)	Resistance (Ω)
100			
90			
80			
70			
60			
50			
40			
30			
20			
10			

Graph 1

Activity 2 calculations

Check your understanding

1. Describe the relationship between the length of a wire and its resistance.   [1 mark]

   ....

2. Use your graph to state whether this relationship is **proportional** or **directly proportional**.

   Justify your answer.   [2 marks]

   ....

   ....

3. By adding a bulb to your circuit, you increase the resistance.

   Explain why this stops the wire from overheating.   [2 marks]

   ....

   ....

Exam-style questions

1. State the units for potential difference, current and resistance.   [2 marks]

   a. Potential difference (*V*)   ....

   b. Current (*I*)   ....

   c. Resistance (*R*)   ....

2. State the equation that links potential difference, current and resistance.   [1 mark]

   ....

3. Current is affected by the resistance of a wire.

   Describe what happens to the current as the resistance of a wire is increased.   [1 mark]

   ....

Some components have a constant resistance. If we double the potential difference, the current doubles. We call these components **ohmic**. Other components do not have a constant resistance – increasing the potential difference might alter the current flow but it does not change proportionately. These are called **non-ohmic**. We can tell which are which by testing them, plotting graphs of the data and looking at the shape of the graph.

Learning outcomes	Maths skills required	Formulae
• Use a range of circuits to safely gather data. • Make measurements using ammeters and voltmeters. • Use a graph to draw conclusions. • Identify variables that need to be kept constant in order to ensure validity of results	• Plot two variables from experimental data. • Interpret graphs that represent a linear relationship.	• potential difference (V) = current (A) × resistance (Ω)

Apparatus list

- 0–12 V variable power supply and connecting leads
- voltmeter or multimeter to measure V
- ammeter or multimeter to measure A
- milliammeter or multimeter to measure mA (you may need this if you have a diode only capable of small currents)
- variable resistor (for example, 10 Ω, 5 A)
- resistor (for example, 100 Ω, 1 W)

- filament lamp (for example, 12 V, 24 W)
- diode
- additional protective resistor (for example, 10 Ω) (optional) – you may need this to ensure your diode does not 'blow'; attach this in series with your diode if advised to by your teacher or science technician
- a switch to turn the circuit on and off (optional)

Safety notes

- Don't turn the power pack up too high! It will damage the components.
- The filament bulb and other components might get hot. Take care not to burn yourself on them.
- Check the equipment before use. If it appears damaged, don't use it.

Common mistakes

- Do not use a.c. in these experiments, use d.c. instead.
- It is **really** hard to set the potential difference to round numbers (e.g. 2 V, 3 V, 4 V) using the variable resistor. If you are struggling, you can take out the variable resistor and use the power pack values for potential difference – even though the potential difference may not be **exactly** what it says on the dial, the amount it increases by is the same each time you turn it up; the intervals are the same.

Diode problems – Activity 3

- If you are getting a current of 0 A or a very low current that doesn't increase at all, it might be that your leads are already switched for negative values. Try swapping them round.
- Don't forget the protective resistor if you have a low current diode! Without the protective resistor, you will blow the diode and then you can't get any results.

Methods

Read these instructions carefully before you start work.

There are three activities to complete.

Activity 1 – Resistor

1. Construct the circuit as shown in **Figure 1**.

2. For different settings of the variable resistor, record the values of current and potential difference. Take five pairs of readings. Turn off the powerpack in between readings to ensure the temperature of the resistor is kept constant.

3. Record the values in **Table 1**.

4. Swap the leads at the power supply (i.e. connect it so that the potential difference is negative).

5. Take readings as before and record them in **Table 1**.

Figure 1

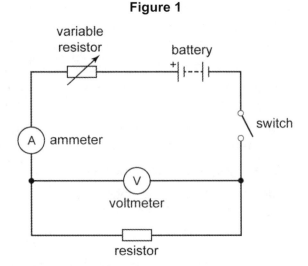

Activity 2 – Filament lamp

1. Construct the circuit as shown in **Figure 2**.

2. For different settings of the variable resistor, record the values of current and potential difference. Take at least five pairs of readings.

3. Record the values in **Table 2**.

4. Swap the leads at the power supply (i.e. connect it so that the potential difference is negative).

5. Take readings as before and record them in **Table 2**.

Figure 2

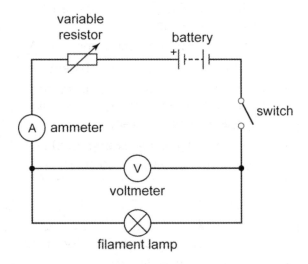

Activity 3 – Diodes

1. Construct the circuit as shown in **Figure 3** using an ammeter if you have a high-current diode, or a milliammeter if you have a low-current diode.

2. This activity may be tricky. Take any readings you can get, even if they are really close together. The range of possible results for this component can be tiny! After you have a few readings, try altering the setting on the variable resistor. Take four further pairs of readings, if possible.

3. Swap the leads at the power supply (i.e. connect it so that the potential difference is negative).

4. Take at least five pairs of readings as before.

5. Record all the values in **Table 3**.

Figure 3

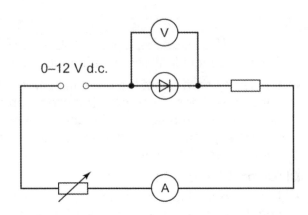

Plot graphs of current against potential difference for each component. Draw lines of best fit. Make sure you label your graphs clearly for each component.

Record your results

Table 1

Resistor at constant temperature

	Potential difference (V)	Current (A)
Positive values		
	0	0
Negative values		

Table 2

Filament bulb

Potential difference (V)	Current (A)
0	0

Table 3

Diode

Potential difference (V)	Current (A)
0	0

Check your understanding

1. Look at your graphs and describe the relationship between current and potential difference for a resistor at a constant temperature. [1 mark]

....

2. Explain why the power supply should be turned off between readings. [2 marks]

....

....

3. Calculate the resistance of your resistor at a constant temperature. [2 marks]

....

....

4. Describe how you can improve the accuracy of this calculated result. [2 marks]

....

....

Exam-style questions

1. When the potential difference across a filament lamp is 6.6 V, the current is 0.3 A.

   Calculate the resistance. Give the correct unit. [2 marks]

....

....

2. A student wants to investigate how the current through a diode affects its resistance.

   Describe how the student could use a circuit to investigate how current through a diode affects the resistance of the diode. [6 marks]

....

....

....

....

....

....

4.3.1.1 Density

Scientists learnt how to measure density in an interesting way. Density is worked out from knowing the mass of an object and the volume it occupies. Measuring the volume is easy enough if the object is a regular shape such as a cube, but what if it was, say, a crown?

This problem was given to Archimedes, a clever scientist who lived thousands of years ago in Greece. The king had ordered a new crown to be made but suspected the craftsman had mixed a cheaper metal with the gold. Measuring the density would reveal whether the gold was pure or not, but how could the volume be found?

Archimedes realised that by carefully immersing the crown in a full can of water, the water that overflowed would have the same volume as the crown.

You are going to carry out an investigation into the density of different shaped objects – both regular and irregular – and of a liquid, gathering data for mass and volume.

Learning outcomes	Maths skills required	Formulae
• Calculate the density of regularly and irregularly shaped objects. • Take multiple readings to calculate a mean. • Measure length, volume and mass accurately using appropriate equipment.	• Calculate mean values from repeated measurements. • Calculate volumes of cuboids. • Record results to calculations using an appropriate number of significant figures.	• density = mass ÷ volume • volume of a cuboid = length × width × height

Apparatus list
• 50 cm³ measuring cylinder   • balance (mass) • 100 cm³ measuring cylinder   • a selection of regularly shaped rectangular objects • 250 cm³ beaker   • ruler, micrometer or Vernier callipers • water • modelling clay

Safety notes
• Be careful when using water and the electronic balance.

Common mistakes
• In Activity 2, make sure your modelling clay object isn't too big, if the measuring cylinder overflows, you won't be able to measure the increased volume accurately. • If your measuring cylinders are too small, your school might have Eureka cans that you can use. If you use Eureka cans, you only need to fill in column 1 – **Mass (g)**, column 4 – **Volume of modelling clay (cm³)** and column 5 – **Density (g/cm³)** of **Table 2**.

Method

Read these instructions carefully before you start work.

There are three activities for this practical.

Activity 1 – Calculating the density of a regularly shaped object

1. Measure the length, width and height of a regularly shaped object using an appropriate piece of equipment for measuring. Record the dimensions in **Table 1**, using an appropriate number of significant figures.

2. Calculate the volume using the formula: volume = length × width × height

    Record the volume in **Table 1** using an appropriate number of significant figures.

3. Measure the mass of the object using the balance. Record the mass in **Table 1**.

4. Calculate the density using the formula: density = mass ÷ volume

    Record the density in **Table 1**.

5. Repeat for two more rectangular objects.

Activity 2 – Calculating the density of an irregularly shaped object

1. Fill the measuring cylinder to 50 cm^3 with water from the beaker. Record the exact volume in **Table 2**.

2. Take a blob of modelling clay and squeeze it into any shape you like, so long as it will fit into the measuring cylinder.

3. Measure and record the mass of your modelling clay shape in **Table 2**.

4. Carefully slide the modelling clay shape into the water by tilting the measuring cylinder at an angle. Make sure the modelling clay is totally covered.

5. Measure the new volume and record this in **Table 2**.

6. Calculate the volume change and record this in **Table 2**. This is the volume of the modelling clay shape.

7. Calculate the density of the modelling clay shape by using the formula: density = mass ÷ volume

    Record the density in **Table 2**, using an appropriate number of significant figures.

8. Repeat this twice more for different sizes of modelling clay shapes, also recording your results in **Table 2**.

9. Calculate a mean value for the density of the modelling clay.

Activity 3 – Calculating the density of a liquid

1. Measure the mass of an empty 50 cm^3 measuring cylinder. Record the mass in **Table 3**.

2. Fill the measuring cylinder to 50 cm^3 with water, or a different liquid. Record the exact volume in **Table 3**.

3. Measure the mass of the measuring cylinder and the liquid. Record the mass in **Table 3**.

4. Calculate the mass of the liquid by calculating the difference between your two measurments, and record the measurement in **Table 3**.

5. Calculate the density of the liquid by using the formula: density = mass ÷ volume.

Record your results

Table 1 – Density of regular objects

Object	Length (cm)	Width (cm)	Height (cm)	Volume (cm³)	Mass (g)	Density (g/cm³)

Table 2 – Density of irregular objects

Mass (g)	Volume without modelling clay (cm³)	Volume with modelling clay (cm³)	Volume of modelling clay (cm³)	Density (g/cm³)
Mean				

Table 3 – Density of a liquid

Mass of the empty cylinder (g)	Volume of liquid (cm³)	Masss of cylinder plus liquid (cm³)	Mass of liquid (g)	Density (g/cm³)

Check your understanding

1. In your investigation, you calculated the density of modelling clay.

   a. Explain why it was important to try more than one shape. [1 mark]

   ....

   b. Predict the effect of an air bubble trapped inside the modelling clay on the calculated density.

   Give a reason for your prediction. [2 marks]

   ....

   ....

2. A student has a regular cube that is too big to place inside a measuring cylinder.

   a. Suggest a piece of equipment that could be used to calculate the volume of the cube. [1 mark]

....

   b. Describe how this piece of equipment could be used to calculate the volume of the cube. [1 mark]

....

Exam-style questions

1. Petrol is a liquid with a density lower than that of water.

Describe a method to calculate the density of petrol. [4 marks]

....

....

....

....

....

2. A 2.0 m^3 block of aluminium has a mass of 5 400 000 g.

Calculate the density of aluminium in kg/m^3. [2 marks]

....

....

Density of aluminium = ... kg/m^3

3. A 2.0 m^3 block of steel has a density of 7700 kg/m^3.

Calculate the mass of the steel block in kg. [2 marks]

....

....

Mass of steel block = ... kg

4. Explain why aluminium is often used to build aeroplanes, but steel is not.

Use your understanding of density to help you. [2 marks]

....

....

It is easy to make a spring by winding a length of wire around a cylindrical object. You can investigate how springs behave when loaded with a weight. You are going to investigate the relationship between the force applied to stretch a spring and its extension.

Learning outcomes	Maths skills required	Formulae
• Accurately measure the extension of a spring to calculate the spring constant. • Plot a graph of results and identify the limit of proportionality.	• Plot two variables from experimental data. • Interpret graphs that represent a linear relationship. • Calculate the gradient of a graph.	• force = spring constant × extension $F = ke$

Apparatus list

- spring
- set of masses and mass holder appropriate for the spring you are testing
- clamp stand
- ruler
- 1 kg mass to put on base of clamp stand to stabilise it OR a table clamp
- eye protection

Safety notes

- Be careful not to drop the masses on to your foot.

Common mistakes

- Don't confuse length with extension. The extension is the stretched length minus the original length of the spring.
- Try not to stretch the spring when you add and remove masses.

Method

Read these instructions carefully before you start work.

1. Set up the equipment as shown in **Figure 1**, but without any masses or the mass holder on the spring.

2. Measure the length of the spring with no masses attached. Record this length in **Table 1** in the **Length of spring (cm)** column for 0 N. The extension is filled in for you: no force means no extension.

3. Add a mass holder to the end of the spring and measure the length of the spring, using the pointer to improve accuracy.

4. Record the force on the spring and the new length of the spring in **Table 1**; a mass of 100g has a weight of 1N.

   Calculate how much the spring has extended:
   new length – original length for 0 N

Figure 1

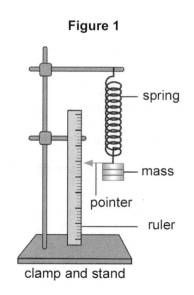

spring

mass

pointer

ruler

clamp and stand

5. Repeat steps **3** and **4**, adding the same amount of mass each time.

6. Stop when your spring shows signs of reaching the limit of proportionality. Make sure you do not overstretch your spring.

7. Plot a graph of your results for force against extension on **Graph 1**.

   Plot force on the *x*-axis and extension on the *y*-axis.

Record your results

Table 1 – Calculating extension

Force on spring (N)	Length of spring (cm)	Extension of spring (cm)
0		0

Graph 1

Check your understanding

1. Look at the graph and describe the relationship between force and extension. [2 marks]

   ....

   ....

2. Identify the limit of proportionality on your graph. [1 mark]

   ....

3. Suggest an improvement to this experiment that would improve the accuracy of your results. [1 mark]

....

....

4. Use $F = ke$ to calculate the spring constant of your spring. [1 mark]

....

....

Exam-style questions

1. **Graph 2** shows the results for an experiment investigating the extension of a spring.

Graph 2

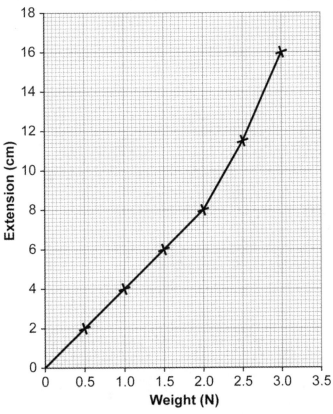

a. State the extension beyond which the limit of proportionality is exceeded. [1 mark]

....

b. State the formula linking force, extension and spring constant. [1 mark]

....

c. Use the graph to calculate the spring constant of the spring.

Give your answer in N/m. [3 marks]

....

....

....

....

....

....

d. The formula for calculating elastic potential energy is:

elastic potential energy = 0.5 × spring constant × extension^2

Calculate the amount of energy stored as elastic potential energy when the spring has 1 N of force applied to it.

Give the unit for your answer. [4 marks]

....

....

....

....

....

....

....

There is a very important relationship between force, mass and acceleration. This is a fundamental idea in Physics. It is possible to demonstrate the relationship using fairly straightforward apparatus and analysing the results with care.

You are going to carry out a practical investigation into Newton's second law.

Newton's second law of motion says that if a force accelerates an object, the acceleration is **directly proportional** to the force and **inversely proportional** to the mass of the object. You should be able to analyse your results to see whether they show this relationship.

Learning outcomes	Maths skills required	Formulae
• Make accurate measurements of length, mass and time. • Take multiple readings to calculate a mean. • Identify the independent and dependent variables, and the control variables.	• Find a mean. • Use an appropriate number of significant figures.	• speed = $\dfrac{\text{distance}}{\text{time}}$ • acceleration = $\dfrac{\text{change in velocity}}{\text{time taken}}$

Apparatus list
• light gate linked to a computer • trolley with U-shaped interrupt card attached • pulley on clamp • string   • four 100 g masses and 100 g mass holder • stopwatch • box or tray to catch masses in • pencil, chalk or masking tape to mark the intervals

Safety notes
• Be careful when masses are released from the bench as they might land on your feet. • Prevent the trolley and interrupt card from falling off the bench.

Common mistakes
• Make sure you have your light gate and interrupt card at the right height. Ask your teacher for help if you don't know how to set them up. • In Activity 1, make sure you don't change the mass of the system. Masses that aren't on the hook adding to the force accelerating the trolley need to be attached to/on the trolley. This makes sure that the total mass experiencing acceleration remains the same throughout your experiment. • Don't forget that some mass hooks already have a mass of 100 g attached. Ask your teacher if you are unsure of the masses you have. • For Method 2 in Activity 1, don't forget you will need to first calculate the average speed of the trolley in each segment. Then to find the acceleration of the trolley between segments find the change of speed from one segment to the next and the time the trolley took to speed up from one segment to the next.

Method

Read these instructions carefully before you start work.

There are two activities to complete.

Activity 1 – Measuring the effect of force on acceleration at constant mass

There are two different methods for this practical. Choose the method that best suits the apparatus available.

Method 1 – Using light gates

1. Set up the equipment as shown in **Figure 1** or similar if your light gate equipment is different.

Figure 1

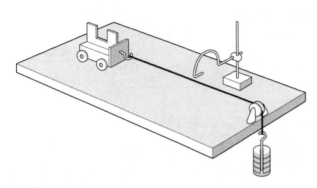

2. Measure the width of each segment of the interrupt car and enter the values into the datalogging software.

3. Place 400 g of mass on the trolley. Add 100 g of mass (1 N of force) to the hook and hold the trolley in place at the 'start line'.

4. Record the acceleration of the trolley as it passes through the light gate using the datalogger. Record this result in **Table 1** using the following headings.

Force (N)	Acceleration (m/s²)			
	First reading	Second reading	Third reading	Mean

   Repeat twice more, record your results and calculate the mean acceleration.

5. Take a 100 g mass **off the** trolley and add it to the hook so there is now a force of 2 N. Measure the acceleration for this force.

6. Repeat step **4** up to 5 N of force so all five 100 g masses are on the hook and there are no masses on the trolley.

Method 2 – Using stopwatches

1. Set up the equipment as shown in **Figure 2**.

Figure 2

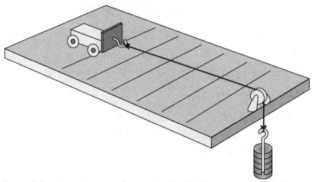

2. Mark at least five straight lines across the surface. They should be an equal distance apart (e.g. 20cm).

3. Place 300 g of mass on the trolley. Add 100 g of mass (1 N of force) to the hook and hold the trolley at the start line.

4. Start the stopwatch as you release the trolley and press 'lap' as the trolley passes each line on the surface. Record the times at each distance for the applied force of 1 N in **Table 1** using the following headings.

Distance travelled (cm)	Time (s)			
	1N	2N	3N	4N

5. Take a 100 g mass **off the** trolley and add it to the hook so the applied force is now 2 N. Measure the time taken for each segment again.

6. Repeat step **4** up to 4 N of force so all four 100 g masses are on the hook and there are no masses on the trolley.

7. Calculate the acceleration of your trolley in each segment, for each force. You could record the calculated acceleration in **Table 1** in a different colour next to the time at each distance.

Activity 2 – Measuring the effect of mass on acceleration with a constant force

1. Set up the equipment as you did in **Activity 1**,

2. Using your results from **Activity 1,** choose an appropriate number of masses to hang on the string to accelerate the trolley along the track.

3. Place 400 g of mass on the trolley. Add your chosen mass to the hook and hold the trolley in place at the 'start line'.

4. Repeat your experiment as you did in **Activity 1** and record your results in **Table 2.**

   If you followed **Method 1** in **Activity 1**, use the following headings for **Table 2.**

Mass of car (g)	Acceleration (m/s²)			
	First reading	Second reading	Third reading	Mean

   If you followed **Method 2** in **Activity 1**, use the following headings for **Table 2.**

Distance travelled (cm)	Mass of car (g)			

5. Repeat your experiment again with fewer masses on the car. Make sure you don't change the mass hanging on the string. This is kept constant to keep the force applied to the trolley constant.

Record your results

Table 1

Table 2

Check your understanding

1. State the independent and dependent variables in Activity 1, and in Activity 2. [3 marks]

   Independent variable ....

   Dependent variable ....

2. **a.** List two variables that were controlled in Activity 1. [2 marks]

   ....

   ....

   b. Explain why it is important that a pulley is used as the string runs over the edge of the bench. [1 mark]

   ....

   ....

Exam-style questions

1. A student investigated the effect of changing the force on the acceleration of a trolley by adding masses to a string attached to a trolley. As the masses fell, the trolley was pulled forward and the student used two light gates to measure the trolley's speed at two points and the time taken to go between the two points. The student used this data to calculate the acceleration.

   The results are shown in **Table 2**.

   Table 2

Force (N)	Acceleration (m/s^2)
1	0.5
2	0.9
3	1.4
4	2.1
5	2.5
6	3.0
7	3.6
8	4.1

   a. Plot the results for force against acceleration on **Graph 1**. [3 marks]

Graph 1

b. Describe the relationship between force and acceleration. [2 marks]

....

....

c. Use the graph to find the acceleration if 3.5 N of force was applied to the trolley. [1 mark]

....

d. **HT** Inertial mass is a measure of how difficult it is to change the velocity of an object.

Use the results of the experiment to calculate the inertial mass of the trolley. Give your answer to 1 significant figure. [3 marks]

....

....

....Inertial mass of the trolley = ... kg

By careful observation and measurement we can measure and calculate the **wavelength** and **frequency** of the waves and then work out their **speed**. We can use a piece of equipment called a ripple tank to explore waves thorugh water. A strobe light can be used to 'freeze' the movement of the waves for making certain measurements. You are going to investigate how to measure the speed of water waves and the speed of waves along a stretched string.

Learning outcomes	Maths skills required	Formulae
• Carry out an investigation to measure the speed of a wave. • Evaluate the method. • Understand how to identify any anomalous results.	• Substitute numerical values into algebraic equations using appropriate units for physical quantities.	• wave speed = frequency × wavelength

Apparatus list

Activity 1
- ripple tank
- strobe light
- low-voltage power pack
- A 5 W or 6 W signal generator
- wooden bridge
- vibration generator

Activity 2
- stretched string or elastic cord
- 100 g and 10 g masses and hangers
- pulley on clamp
- stopwatch
- metre ruler
- eye protection

Safety notes

- Do not handle the power pack, plug or socket with wet hands.
- Be careful with water and electrical pieces of equipment.
- Let your teacher know if you will be affected by stroboscopic or flashing lights.

Common mistakes

- If you are struggling to measure the length of water waves in Activity 1, use a camera or phone to take a photo of the wave patterns next to a ruler.
- If you are struggling to produce a stable wave pattern in the stretched string or elastic, ask your teacher for help.
- In Activity 2 the distance between two points on the string where the vibration amplitude is zero is *half* a wavelength, so the wavelength is *twice* this distance.

Method

Read these instructions carefully before you start work.

There are two activities for you to complete.

Activity 1 – Wave speed through a liquid

1. Set up the ripple tank as shown in **Figure 1**.

2. Count the number of waves that pass a given point every 10 seconds. Record the results in **Table 1**.

3. Measure the length of 10 waves. Record the results in **Table 1**.

4. Change the frequency and take the measurements again.

5. Repeat this until you have at least six sets of results. Find the wave frequency and wavelength for each set of results.

6. Calculate the speed of the waves for each set of results using the equation:
   wave speed = frequency × wavelength

Figure 1

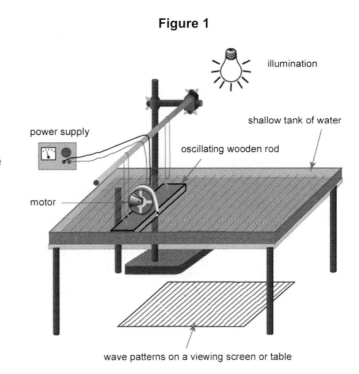

Activity 2 – Wave speed through a solid

Figure 2

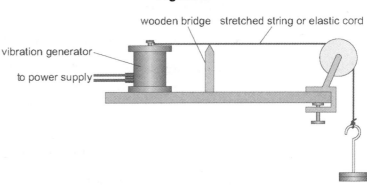

1. Set up the equipment as shown in **Figure 2**.

2. Put on your eye protection. Turn on the vibration generator. The attached string (or elastic) will start to vibrate up and down.

3. If you cannot see a stable wave pattern along the string, adjust the length of the string which vibrates by slowly moving the wooden bridge away from the vibration generator until it looks like the waves are not moving and you can see clear standing waves. If you cannot see any waves, add another mass to the hanger and then try moving the wooden bridge again.

4. Measure the length of one **wavelength**. Record this in **Table 2**.

5. Record the **frequency** of the signal generator.

6. Calculate the speed of the wave using the equation: wave speed = frequency × wavelength

7. Change the frequency on the signal generator and repeat Steps **3 – 6** twice more.

Record your results

Table 1 – Calculating wave speed in Activity 1

Result	Number of waves in 10 seconds	Wave frequency (number of waves in 1 second)	Length of 10 waves (m)	Wavelength (length of 1 wave) (m)	Speed (m/s)
1					
2					
3					
4					
5					
6					

Table 2 – Calculating wave speed in Activity 2

Wavelength (m)	Frequency (Hz)	Speed (m/s)

Check your understanding

1. The speed of waves through a liquid should be constant for the same liquid depth.

   a. Which, if any, of your results in **Table 1** looks most like it might be an anomalous result? [1 mark]

   ....

   b. Calculate the mean wave speed for your wave speeds in **Table 1**.

      Do not include any anomalous results. [1 mark]

   ....

      Mean wave speed = ... m/s

2. Explain why the method in **Activity 1** asks you to measure the length of 10 waves to calculate the wavelength, rather than just measuring the length of one wave. [1 mark]

   ....

3. Identify one possible source of error in the measurement of wavelength in **Activity 2**. [1 mark]

....

....

Exam-style questions

1. State the units of wave speed, frequency and wavelength. [2 marks]

   a. Wave speed ....

   b. Frequency ....

   c. Wavelength ....

2. State the equation that links wave speed, frequency and wavelength. [1 mark]

....

In this practical you will investigate the reflection of light by different types of surface and the refraction of light by different substances. In the experiment you will trace the path of light refracted and reflected through blocks of two different materials. You will use a ray box to produce a narrow ray of light.

When measuring the angles to do with light rays, remember to measure the angles from the normal, the line drawn at right angles to the surface where the ray meets the other medium.

Learning outcomes	Maths skills required	Formulae
• Identify incident, reflected and refracted rays and angles. • Accurately measure angles of incidence, reflection and refraction. • Draw conclusions from your results.	• Measure angles.	• angle of incidence = angle of reflection

Apparatus list

- clear acrylic block
- clear glass block
- any other clear blocks available
- ray box with a slit
- protractor
- ruler
- pencil

Safety notes

- Be careful of sharp edges on chipped glass blocks.
- Do not knock glass blocks together as sharp chips may fly off.
- Ray boxes may get very hot, so take care not to burn yourself.

Common mistakes

- Don't forget to draw a pencil line along the edge of the block, and to draw the normal perpendicular (at a right angle) to this line.

Methods

Read these instructions carefully before you start work.

There are two activities for you to complete.

Activity 1 – Refraction

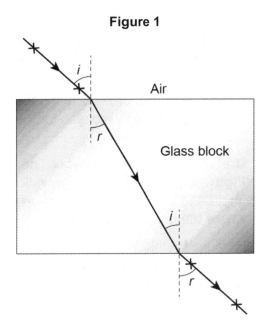

Figure 1

1. Draw around a glass block in the space below and angle the ray box so that the ray of light enters one long side of the block and exits the other, as in **Figure 1**.

2. Draw at least two crosses along the path of the ray entering the block and also for the ray exiting the block.

3. Without moving the block, carefully draw the two normals using a dashed line, as in **Figure 1**. These should be perpendicular (at right angles) to the edge of the block, at the points where the ray enters and leaves the block.

4. Remove the block and draw straight lines with a pencil and ruler to join up the crosses for the rays exiting and entering the block. Extend the lines so they go up to the edge of the block.

5. Using a ruler, connect the two lines showing the path of the light through the block. Add arrows to the lines to show the direction of the light.

6. Using a protractor, measure the angles of incidence (i) and the angles of refraction (r).

7. Record your results in **Table 1**.

8. Repeat using either a different material for the block or different angles of incidence.

Activity 2 – Reflection

1. Draw around a glass block in the space below and angle the ray box so that the ray of light hits one long side of the block and is reflected, as shown in **Figure 2**.

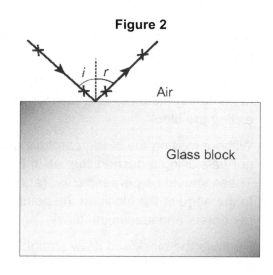

Figure 2

2. Draw at least two crosses along the path of the ray hitting the block and also for the ray reflected by the block.

3. Draw a normal using a dashed line, as in **Figure 2**. This should be perpendicular (at right angles) to the edge of the block, at the point where the ray meets the block.

4. Remove the block and draw straight lines with a pencil and ruler to join up the crosses for the lines hitting and being reflected by the block. Extend the lines so they go up to the edge of the block.

5. Add arrows to the lines to show the direction of the light.

6. Using a protractor, measure the angle of incidence (i) and the angle of reflection (r). Record your results in **Table 2**.

7. Repeat using a different material for the block and different angles of incidence.

Record your results

Table 1 – Refraction

| Material of block | Ray entering the block | | Ray exiting the block | |
	Angle of incidence in degrees	Angle of refraction in degrees	Angle of incidence in degrees	Angle of refraction in degrees

Table 2 – Reflection

Material of block	Angle of incidence in degrees	Angle of reflection in degrees

Plot a graph of your results for one of the blocks from Table 2 of angle of reflection against angle of incidence and draw a line of best fit. Plot this on a sheet of graph paper and stick into your lab book. Plot the results for the two materials on the same axes, and use error bars for the plotted points.

Check your understanding

1. State the relationship between the angle of incidence and the angle of reflection. Use data from your experiment to support your answer. [2 marks]

    ....

    ....

2. Explain why it is important to have a narrow ray of light exiting the ray box when carrying out these experiments. [1 mark]

....

3. A student wanted to extend **Activity 1** by using a beaker full of water to measure the angle of refraction for light passing from air to water.

Explain why using a beaker would not be suitable for this experiment. [2 marks]

....

....

Exam-style questions

1. A ray of light hits a plane mirror at an angle of incidence of 40°.

    a. State the angle of reflection. [1 mark]

    ....

    b. Draw the incident ray and the reflected ray on **Figure 3**.

    Include the following labels. [4 marks]
    i.   Incident ray
    ii.   Reflected ray
    iii. Angle of incidence
    iv.   Angle of reflection
    v.   Normal

Figure 3

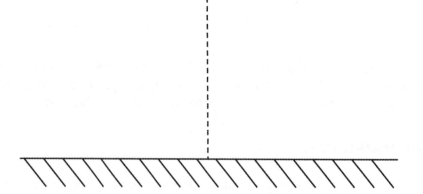

All objects give off infrared radiation and the warmer it is, the more quickly it emits radiation. However, the colour of an object also affects how much radiation it emits. If we want a radiator to work as well as possible, the colour matters.

You will investigate how the nature of a surface affects the amount of infrared radiation emitted or absorbed.

Learning outcomes	Maths skills required
• Identify independent, dependent and control variables in an investigation. • Carry out a practical investigation to find out how the nature of a surface affects the amount of infrared radiation it emits. • Measure temperature accurately.	• Display experimental data in a suitable table and chart.

Apparatus list	
• Leslie cube • thermometer • heatproof mat • ruler • kettle full of water • infrared detector	• three test tubes; one painted black, one painted white, one covered in foil • three thermometers, one in each tube • test tube rack • a 250 W bulb and power source • 10 cm^3 measuring cylinder • stopwatch

Safety notes
• Be careful with the hot water! Make sure you do not carry containers of hot water across the lab. Take the kettle to your desk and boil the water there if possible. • **Don't** pick up the Leslie cube when it is full of hot water. It will be very, very hot. • Do not touch the bulb! It will be very hot even after it has been turned off.

Common mistakes
• In Activity 1, you should keep the sensor the same distance from each face of the cube. • In Activity 2, you should keep the light bulb the same distance from each test tube.

Method

Read these instructions carefully before you start work.

There are two activities to complete.

Activity 1 – Investigating the amount of infrared radiation radiated from different surfaces

1. Place the Leslie cube onto a heatproof mat.

2. Fill the cube with very hot water and replace the lid of the cube.

3. **DO NOT TOUCH THE LESLIE CUBE.**

4. Place the infrared detector 5 cm from the surface, as shown in **Figure 1**, and measure the amount of infrared radiation radiated from each surface.

5. Measure the temperature using the thermometer. Record your results in **Table 1**.

Figure 1

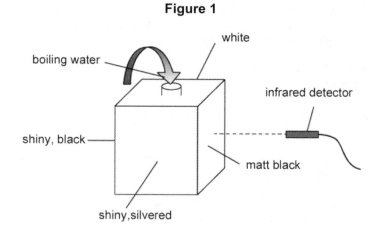

6. Measure the amount of radiation emitted by the other surface types. Work quickly so the temperature of the water is the same for each measurement.

7. Draw a bar graph of your results in **Graph 1**.

Activity 2 – Investigating the amount of infrared radiation absorbed by different surfaces

1. Measure 10 cm³ of cold water using the measuring cylinder and pour into the black painted test tube. Repeat for the white painted test tube and the one wrapped in aluminium foil.

2. Place the bulb 5-10 cm away from the test tubes, and switch it on.

3. Take the temperature of the water, record in **Table 2** and start the stop watch.

4. After 5 minutes, take the temperature of the water again and record the temperature in **Table 2**. Repeat every 2 minutes up to 10 minutes.

Record your results

Table 1 – Amount of infrared radiation emitted

Surface type	Temperature of water (°C)	Reading on infrared detector

Table 2 – Effect of coloured surface on absorption of infrared radiation

Surface	Temperature of water (°C)					
	0 mins	2 mins	4 mins	6 mins	8 mins	10 mins
Black paint						
White paint						
Aluminium foil						

Graph 1

Check your understanding

1. State the independent variable and the dependent variable in **Activity 1**. [2 marks]

   Independent variable ....

   Dependent variable ....

2. List two control variables in **Activity 1**. [2 marks]

....

....

3. Describe how you could improve the accuracy of **Activity 2**. [2 marks]

....

....

Exam-style questions

1. A student wants to find out if different coloured surfaces emit different amounts of radiation when they are at the same temperature. Her hypothesis is that the darker the colour of a surface, the more infrared radiation is emitted from it.

   She has the following equipment:
   - four test tubes that have been painted different colours: white, grey, black and unpainted (as a control)
   - an infrared detector
   - a kettle
   - a thermometer.

   Plan an experiment to allow the student to test her hypothesis. [6 marks]

   ....

   ....

   ....

   ....

   ....

   ....

2. As a method of measuring the amount of infrared radiation emitted, the student suggests measuring the temperature at a set distance from each test tube.

   Suggest a reason why this may not be as accurate as using an infrared detector. [1 mark]

   ....

   ....

3. The student's results show that the material the test tube is covered in does affect the amount of radiation emitted. Suggest why. [1 mark]

   ....

Equations

It is important to be able to recall and apply the following equations using standard units. Shaded equations are higher tier only.

Equation number	Word equation	Symbol equation
1	weight = mass × gravitational field strength	$W = mg$
2	work done = force × distance (along the line of action of the force)	$W = Fs$
3	force applied to a spring = spring constant × extension	$F = ke$
4	moment of a force = force × distance (normal to direction of force)	$M = Fd$
5	pressure = $\dfrac{\text{force normal to a surface}}{\text{area of that surface}}$	$p = \dfrac{F}{A}$
6	distance travelled = speed × time	$s = vt$
7	acceleration = $\dfrac{\text{change in velocity}}{\text{time taken}}$	$a = \dfrac{\Delta v}{t}$
8	resultant force = mass × acceleration	$F = ma$
9	momentum = mass × velocity	$p = mv$
10	kinetic energy = 0.5 × mass × (speed)²	$E_k = \frac{1}{2}mv^2$
11	gravitational potential energy = mass × gravitational field strength × height	$E_p = mgh$
12	power = $\dfrac{\text{energy transferred}}{\text{time}}$	$P = \dfrac{E}{t}$
13	power = $\dfrac{\text{work done}}{\text{time}}$	$P = \dfrac{W}{t}$
14	efficiency = $\dfrac{\text{useful output energy transfer}}{\text{total input energy transfer}}$	
15	efficiency = $\dfrac{\text{useful power output}}{\text{total power input}}$	
16	wave speed = frequency × wavelength	$v = f\lambda$
17	charge flow = current × time	$Q = It$
18	potential difference = current × resistance	$V = IR$
19	power = potential difference × current	$P = VI$
20	power = (current)² × resistance	$P = I^2R$
21	energy transferred = power × time	$E = Pt$
22	energy transferred = charge flow × potential difference	$E = QV$
23	density = $\dfrac{\text{mass}}{\text{volume}}$	$\rho = \dfrac{m}{v}$

The following equations will appear on the equations sheet that you are given in the exam. It is important to be able to select and apply the appropriate equation to answer a question correctly.

Equation number	Word equation	Symbol equation
1	pressure due to a column of liquid = height of column × density of liquid × gravitational field strength	$p = h\rho g$
2	(final velocity)² – (initial velocity)² = 2 × acceleration × distance	$v^2 - u^2 = 2as$
3	force = $\dfrac{\text{change in momentum}}{\text{time taken}}$	$F = \dfrac{m\Delta v}{\Delta t}$
4	elastic potential energy = 0.5 × spring constant × (extension)²	$E_e = \frac{1}{2}ke^2$
5	change in thermal energy = mass × specific heat capacity × temperature change	$\Delta E = mc\Delta\theta$
6	magnification = $\dfrac{\text{image height}}{\text{object height}}$	
7	period = $\dfrac{1}{\text{frequency}}$	
8	force on a conductor (at right angles to a magnetic field) = magnetic flux density × current × length	$F = BIl$
9	thermal energy for a change of state = mass × specific latent heat	$E = mL$
10	$\dfrac{\text{potential difference across primary coil}}{\text{potential difference across secondary coil}} = \dfrac{\text{number of turns in primary coil}}{\text{number of turns in secondary coil}}$	$\dfrac{V_p}{V_s} = \dfrac{n_p}{n_s}$
11	potential difference across primary coil × current in primary coil = potential difference across secondary coil × current in secondary coil	$V_s I_s = V_p I_p$
12	For gases: pressure × volume = constant	$pV = \text{constant}$

For 6 mark method questions you will need to consider:
0 marks: No relevant content | **1-2 marks:** Simple statements are made, Some understanding is demonstrated, Some scientific techniques and procedures are relevant, Lacks logical structure, Valid results cannot be produced | **3-4 marks:** Majority of method is present in detail, Reasonable understanding is demonstrated, Most scientific techniques and procedures are relevant, Mostly logical sequence but some may be illogical and not detailed, Valid results may be produced | **5-6 marks:** Coherent method is present in detail, Good understanding is demonstrated, Broad understanding of scientific techniques and procedures, Logical sequence to method, Valid results can be produced

4.1.1.3 Specific heat capacity

Check your understanding

1. to ensure that the entire mass of the water is heated evenly [1]
2. a. 69 °C (69.3 °C also allowed) [2]
   b. Any one from: [1]
      - misreading of thermometer
      - fault with equipment
3. The thermal energy from the heating element may be transferred to the surrounding air rather than to the block of metal. [1]
4. balance (accept scale) [1]
   measuring cylinder [1]
   thermometer [1]

Exam-style questions

1. a. Your graph should look something like this:

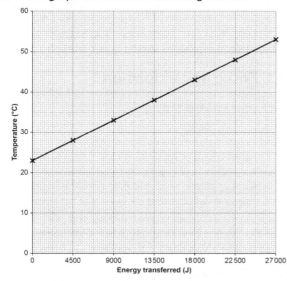

   1 mark for plotting 1 or 2 correct points [1]
   1 mark for all 3 points correctly plotted [1]
   1 mark for line of best fit [1]

   b. gradient of line = 30/27 000 = 0.0011 [1]
   (allow a mark for any other set of values that give a gradient of 0.0011)
   specific heat capacity = 1/(1 × 0.0011)
   = 909.1 [1]
2. Copper would heat up the fastest. [1]
   As it has the lowest specific heat capacity it needs less energy to raise 1 kg by 1 °C. [1]

4.1.2.1 Thermal insulation

Check your understanding

1. a. All of the curves fall quickly at first [1]
      and then begin to level out (at room temperature). [1]
      (Alternative answers depending on your graph could be: a steady decrease at first, [1]
      and then less of a decrease.) [1]
   b. Your answer will depend on your own data: use correctly chosen data from your graph, (e.g. the difference in temperature at 0 and 20 minutes) for number of layers that would be a good choice; [1]
      then compare the difference in temperature to a number of layers that would be a bad choice [1]
      a comment that there is a point at which using additional layers does not give any further benefit. [1]
2. So that valid comparisons can be made of the different materials. [1]
   Because volume of water is a variable – a larger volume of water would take longer to cool. [1]
3. Advise that the student uses a high number of layers, [1]
   as this would slow thermal energy transfer from the environment to the ice cream,
   a comment that there is a point at which using additional layers does not give any further benefit (no additional reduction of energy transfer). [1]

Exam-style questions

1. a. Your answer should include: [6]
   Method
   - Fill a beaker with an amount of water.
   - Use the same amount of water each time.
   - Water should be hot/boiling/at 90 °C.
   - Surround the beaker with one type of insulation.
   - Measure the temperature at the start.
   - Measure the temperature every hour for 5 hours.
   - Repeat for all other insulation types.
   Safety precautions
   - Wear eye protection.
   - Be careful with boiling water.
   - Any other valid point.
   b. because 25 °C is room temperature [1]

4.2.1.3 Resistance

Check your understanding

1. As the length of the wire increases, the resistance also increases. [1]
2. The relationship is directly proportional [1]
   as it is a straight line that passes through the origin. [1]
3. If the resistance is higher, then the current will be lower. [1]
   A lower current passing through a wire will mean it

doesn't get as hot / less energy will be transferred as thermal energy. [1]

Exam-style questions

1. **a.** Potential difference (V) = V (volts)
   b. Current (I) = A (amperes, amps)
   c. Resistance (R) = Ω (ohms) [2]
      2 marks for all three correct;
      1 mark for two or one correct
2. $V = IR$
   resistance = potential difference ÷ current
   1 mark for either version [1]
3. As resistance increases, current decreases. [1]

4.2.1.4 I–V characteristics

Check your understanding

1. As potential difference increases, current increases (in both directions). [1]
2. So that the temperature of the resistor is kept constant. [1]
   Resistance increases as temperature increases. [1]
3. Use any pair of values from results table. [1]
   Calculate using $R = V/I$ [1]
4. Repeat each reading. [1]
   Calculate a mean. [1]

Exam-style questions

1. correct substitution into formula: 6.6/0.3 [1]
   resistance = 22 Ω [1]
2. Answer should include: [6]
   - Ammeter used to measure current.
   - Voltmeter used to measure potential difference.
   - Resistance of variable resistor altered to change current in circuit or change potential difference (across diode).
   - Plot a graph of current against potential difference.
   - Resistance (of diode) calculated from pairs of points on the graph, for current in both directions using R = V/
   - Resistance calculated for a large enough range of currents, flowing in both directions.

4.3.1.1 Density

Check your understanding

1. **a.** Any one of the following points:
   - Air could be caught in crevices of a particular shape, displacing more volume.
   - A mean calculated from repeats makes the results more accurate / closer to the true value.
   - Repeats reduce the effect of random error.
   - Anomalous values can be identified and discarded.
   b. The density will be lower. [1]
      The air bubble will cause an increase in volume of the modelling clay blob but not an increase in mass (or negligible increase in mass). [1]
2. **a.** Any one of the following:
   - a ruler
   - Vernier callipers
   - (a large Eureka can) [1]

b. Either of the following points:
   - Measure one side of the cube and calculate (side)^3 or (just in case it isn't a regular cube), multiply the base by the width by the height.
   - (The cube could be submerged in the Eureka can and the volume of water displaced could be measured.) [1]

Exam-style questions

1. 1 mark for each of the following points:
   - Measure the volume of the petrol (e.g. by using a measuring cylinder). [1]
   - Measure the mass of the petrol (e.g. using a digital balance). [1]
   - Account for the mass of the container; measure mass of container and take away from mass of liquid + container. [1]
   - Use the formula: density = mass ÷ volume [1]
2. Density of aluminium = 2700 kg/m^3 [2]
   5 400 000 g = 5400 kg
   5400 ÷ 2.0 = 2700
   2 marks for correct answer; 1 mark for incorrect answer caused by incorrect unit conversion
3. Mass of steel block = 15 400 kg [2]
   Using formula: density = mass ÷ volume, or mass = density × volume
   2.0 × 7700 = 15 400
   2 marks for correct answer; 1 mark for incorrect answer caused by incorrect formula rearrangement
4. Aluminium has a lower density than steel. [1]
   Aluminium is better as it has less mass per cubic metre and so less energy (fuel, force, lift) is needed to raise each cubic metre off the ground. [1]
   (Answer must refer to density – just saying 'because its lighter' or similar is not enough.)

4.5.3 Force and extension

Check your understanding

1. As force increases, extension also increases. [1]
   The relationship is (directly) proportional. [1]
2. Your own result – the point on the graph at which relationship is no longer directly proportional. [1]
3. Repeat the experiment and calculate the mean. [1]
4. Your answer will depend on your results – correctly calculated for a pair of values when the relationship is directly proportional or calculated using gradient of the graph (units are not required). [1]

Exam-style questions

1. **a.** 8 cm [1]
   b. force = spring constant × extension [1]
   c. The gradient of the graph is 1/spring constant. The spring constant can be found from 1/gradient
      gradient = 4
      1 ÷ 4 = 0.25
      Or, by using $F = ke$, doe pairs of values, for the part of the graph that is linear
      2.0 N ÷ 8.0 cm = 0.25 [1]
      spring constant = 0.25 N/cm [1]
         = 25 N/m [1]
   d. e = 4.0 cm (read from graph) [1]
      4.0 cm = 0.04 m [1]

k = 25 N/m (from part **c**)

E_e = 0.5 × 25 × 0.04^2

E_e = 0.02 [1]

unit = J (joules) [1]

4.5.6.2.2 Acceleration

Check your understanding

1. Independent variable in Activity 1 = force
   Dependent variable in Activity 1 = acceleration
   Independent variable in Activity 2 = mass
   Dependent variable in Activity 2 = acceleration [3]
   3 marks for all four correct; 2 marks for three
   correct; 1 mark for two or one correct
2. **a.** Any two from: [2]
   - mass of the system being accelerated
   - same surface friction
   - same distance between velocity measurements
     (length of U shaped card)
   - any other control variable
   b. EITHER to reduce (effects of) friction OR
   to keep the trolley moving a straight line. [1]

Exam-style questions

1. **a.** See graph below:

   Force (N)

   both axes labelled correctly [1]
   points plotted accurately [1]
   line of best fit drawn [1]
   Subtract 1 mark if axes are reversed –
   dependent variable should be plotted on y-axis
   b. As force increases, acceleration increases. [1]
   The relationship is (directly) proportional. [1]
   c. 1.75 m/s^2 (units are required) [1]
   (anything between 1.5 m/s^2 and 2.0 m/s^2 is
   acceptable)
   d. HT EITHER use $F = ma$
   Take any pair of values from the table for
   force ÷ acceleration, showing working [1]
   answers between 0.45 and 0.53 [1]
   rounded to 0.5 kg (1 significant figure) [1]
   OR
   calculate the gradient of the graph [1]
   gradient between 0.45 and 0.53 [1]
   rounded to 0.5 kg (1 significant figure) [1]

4.6.1.2 Waves

Check your understanding

1. **a.** Your answer will depend on your findings – you
   may notice that one result is far from the rest of
   the spread of results. [1]

b. Your own results. Calculate the sum of all the
wave speeds, excluding any anomalies, and
then divide by the total number of results. [1]
2. EITHER it is easier to measure a larger distance
accurately (i.e. the length of 10 waves) than it
is to measure one shorter wavelength
OR it is harder to define and pick out a single
wave than a set of several waves. [1]
3. Any one from: [1]
   - The movement of the string is very fast / a blur,
     so difficult to decide exactly where to measure
     from.
   - Metre ruler not held parallel to the string, or ruler
     itself is not straight.
   - Parallax error when measuring the length of
     string with the metre ruler.
   - Not converting the distance measured to a
     wavelength (distance could be 1, 2, 3, 4 or 5 half
     wavelengths)

Exam-style questions

1. **a.** Wave speed (v) = m/s (or metres per second
   or m s^{-1})
   b. Frequency (f) = Hz (or hertz)
   c. Wavelength (λ) = m (or metres)
   2 marks for all three correct answers
   1 mark for one or two correct answers
   correct use of letter case required for all three
   (i.e. 'M' is incorrect for metres) [2]
2. wave speed = frequency × wavelength
   $v = f \times \lambda$ [1]
   Word or symbol equation acceptable;
   also accept $f = v/\lambda$ or $\lambda = v/f$

4.6.1.3 Light

Check your understanding

1. Angle of incidence is equal to the angle of
   reflection. [1]
   Any appropriate pair of values from results in Table
   2 where the two values are equal (taking into
   account the small amount of measurement
   uncertainty). [1]
2. Any one from: [1]
   - It is easier to draw an accurate line.
   - It is easier to identify where the centre of the ray
     is.
3. Any two from: [2]
   - The surface of the beaker is curved/convex.
   - It will be difficult (practically) to draw where the
     normal is.
   - It will be difficult (practically) to draw the line /
     measure the angle as the ray leaves the beaker.
   - The ray will get spread out and hard to see
     through the water as the glass has a lensing
     effect.
   - Any other sensible suggestion.

Exam-style questions

1. **a.** 40°
   b. see diagram below:

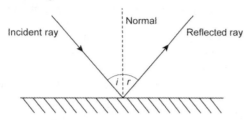

   To gain the 4 marks:
   - rays drawn correctly (must touch each other and the normal at the surface of the mirror, must be straight lines) [1]
   - angles labelled correctly [1]
   - rays labelled correctly (corresponding to correct arrow heads) [1]
   - normal labelled correctly. [1]

4.6.2.2 Radiation and absorption

Check your understanding

1. Independent variable = colour of surface [1]
   Dependent variable = amount of infrared radiation emitted by surface [1]
2. Any two from: [2]
   - distance of infrared detector from surface
   - starting temperature of water
   - amount of water
   - same area of surface
   - any other control variable.
3. Any two from:
   - use a temperature sensor and data logger instead of a glass thermometer to measure temperature [1]
   - take repeat readings (using the same starting water temperature) [1]
   - calculate a mean (excluding any anomalies) [1]

Exam-style questions

1. Answer should include: [6]
   - Boil a kettle.
   - Measure the same amount of boiling water using a measuring cylinder.
   - Put water in the different test tubes; use test tubes that are the same size and shape.
   - Place the infrared detector by the test tubes, the same distance away.
   - Measure the amount of infrared radiation emitted.
   - Repeat for the different test tubes, working quickly so the temperature of the water is the same for each measurement.
   - Take repeat readings using the same initial water temperature, and find the mean (discarding any anomalous results).
2. Thermometers have a poor resolution compared to infrared sensors, so cannot detect small differences in temperature from the different faces. [1]
3. Different materials emit different amounts of radiation. [1]